ON THE JOB

Teams work best when they use each member's strengths to get the job done.

SCHOLASTIC

LITERACY PLACE®

Copyright acknowledgments and credits appear on page 136, which constitutes an extension of this copyright page.

Copyright © 1996 by Scholastic Inc.   All rights reserved.   Printed in the U.S.A.
ISBN 0-590-49103-2

5 6 7 8 9 10   24   02 01 00 99 98 97

Explore
an Ad Agency

Teams work best when they use each member's strengths to get the job done.

Count Me In

Every member of a team is important.

Artists at Work

A team can work together to create works of art.

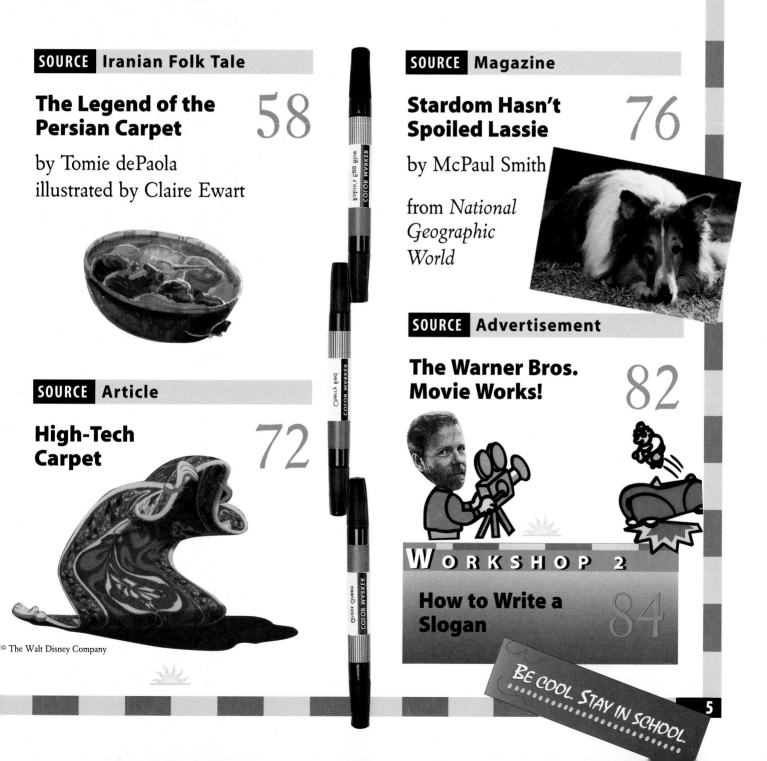

BE COOL. STAY IN SCHOOL.

At Your Service

Some teams work to provide services for others.

Trade Books

The following
books accompany this
On the Job
SourceBook.

Biography

Author/Illustrator

Alvin Ailey

by Andrea Davis Pinkney
illustrated by Brian Pinkney

ALVIN AILEY
Andrea Davis Pinkney
illustrated by Brian Pinkney

■ SCHOLASTIC

Mystery

The Boxcar Children: The Pizza Mystery

created by Gertrude Chandler Warner

#33
The Boxcar Children

THE PIZZA MYSTERY
created by
GERTRUDE CHANDLER WARNER

Science Nonfiction

Author

Finding the Titanic

by Robert D. Ballard

FINDING THE
TITANIC

by Robert D. Ballard,
discoverer of the *Titanic*

■ SCHOLASTIC

Caldecott Award

Historical Fiction

THE CALDECOTT MEDAL

Mirette on the High Wire

by Emily Arnold McCully

MIRETTE
ON THE
HIGH
WIRE
Emily Arnold McCully

■ SCHOLASTIC

Every member of a team is important.

Count Me In

Discover why *Z* is an important member of the alphabet team.

Meet Max Jerome, the art director of an ad agency.

Visit a pasta factory. Then discover spaghetti and meatballs in poetry and art.

WORKSHOP 1

Design an eye-catching cereal box.

THE STORY
OF

THE STORY OF Z

by **Jeanne Modesitt**

illustrated by
Lonni Sue Johnson

One day, the letter Z walked off the alphabet.
"I'm tired of being last in line," she had complained to
X and Y a few minutes earlier. "And my talents just seem
to go unnoticed. Why, I'll bet you I'm the least used
letter of the entire alphabet. It's enough to make
a letter want to leave."

"Z!" gasped X. "How can you say such a thing? You can't leave the alphabet. To do so would be—"

"Mutiny!" cried Y. "Plain and simple mutiny!"

Z tossed her head at Y. "You're just upset because if I were gone, you'd be last in line."

She turned to X. "I've made up my mind. I'm going. Who knows? Maybe I'll start my own alphabet. Coming X?"

X dropped his eyes and said nothing.

"Very well," said Z. "I'm on my own." She sniffed
loudly. "But I guess there's nothing new about **that**,
is there?"

And off she went.

And the world was not the same without her.

For girls no longer understood boys when they
pointed to the sky and said, "Did you see that plane
ig-ag as it oomed by?"

Parents frowned at children when they begged, "Can
we go to the oo and see the ebras?"

And grandchildren laughed at grandparents when they reminded, "Don't forget to ip up your ippers."

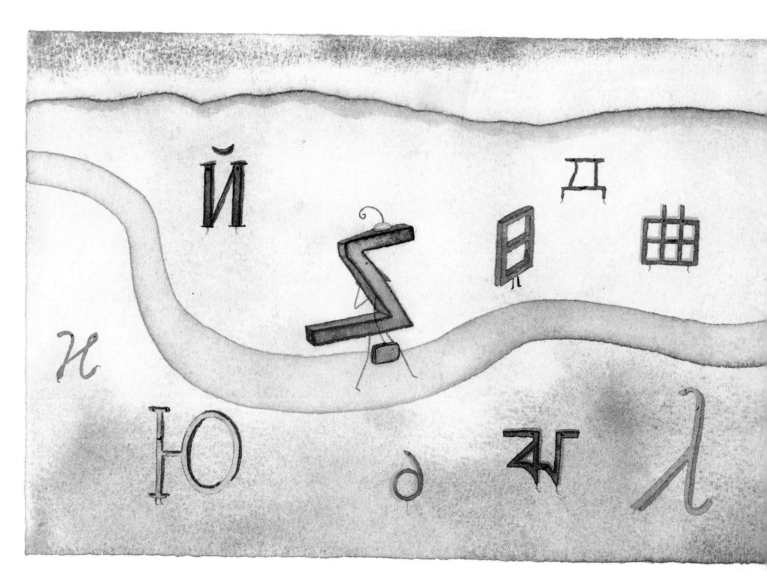

Needless to say, the moment Z left, almost everyone was crying out for her return. Even Y, the most conceited letter of the alphabet, admitted that things had run more smoothly before Z left.

And what did Z think of all this commotion? Well, she was too busy trying to start her own alphabet to even notice it.

But she wasn't having much luck. She couldn't convince any of the letters from the world's different alphabets to join her.

So she began to recruit other types of letters—letters that had never belonged to an alphabet. Unfortunately, such letters rarely do anything for anybody unless there's something in it for them. In fact, the particular letters Z came across were only interested in her idea of starting a new alphabet because they thought the scheme might make them a fast buck, and an easy one at that.

Of course, they didn't tell Z their hidden motives; they simply smiled and nodded and said, "Oh yes, yes, quite a noble plan."

Finally, after Z had made contact with fifteen of these so-called letters, she gathered them together and gave a quick pep talk on how they were about to become the greatest alphabet of all time—with her leading the way, of course.

But the minute she finished her speech and asked,
"Now, who would like to be second?"—the letters began
to push and shove and the whole thing turned into
a brawl.

Z tried to stop the fight but was thrown up into the
air, and landed nearby in a pile of leaves.

Moments later, the letters grew tired of fighting and took off in separate directions. Z was still sitting in the pile of leaves, wondering what to do next, when a street sweeper came along.

"Gad ooks!" he said, as he spotted half of Z sticking out from under the pile of leaves. "What have we here?"

Z looked at the sweeper with a frown. "Gad ooks," she repeated irritably. "What kind of word is that?"

"I'm sorry," said the man. "Let me try again. Gad ooks." Then the man began to cry. "You must forgive me," he said. "Life just hasn't been the same since Z left." The man kept on crying and took out a handkerchief.

"People say she was upset because she was last in line and wasn't used as often as the other letters." The man blew his nose. "I guess she didn't understand how important she was."

Z's attention perked. "Just as important as T?"
she asked.

"Most certainly."

"As important as A or B or that silly Y?"

"Indeed yes."

Z stood up, throwing off her leaves.

"Z!" the man cried. He ran up and hugged her.
"You're back. We've missed you so much. Please, please,
won't you come home?"

Z thought for a moment and then dusted herself off.
"Very well," she said. "I suppose I'd better. Can't have
people running around saying gad ooks to one another."
And off she went . . .

to rejoin her alphabet.

And that night, for the first time in several weeks,

people could finally go to bed in peace.

Max Jerome

Art Director

Visit an *advertising* **agency**
and *meet* **the** team!

What would you do if you made a sneaker that you wanted people to buy? What if you ran a cool new museum and you wanted kids to visit? What would you do? You might call an advertising agency. A special ad team there would find the best way to tell the world about your product.

PROFILE

Name: Max Jerome

Job: art director for an advertising agency

Hometown: New York City

Two words that describe you: funny, honest

Favorite team sport: football

Favorite comic strip: "Hagar the Horrible"

First jobs as a kid: newspaper boy, grocery store clerk

Tools that make your job easier: a computer and posterboard

QUESTIONS
for Max Jerome

Here's how art director *Max Jerome* creates *advertisements* you won't forget.

 Where did you grow up?

 I was born in New York City. Then my family moved to Haiti. Later, we moved to Brooklyn, New York, where I spent most of my childhood.

Q **What is your job?**

A I am an art director for an advertising agency. It's my job to make sure that the ads in magazines and on TV look good.

 Is that a hard job to do by yourself?

A Oh, I couldn't do it alone. I work with a team of writers, designers, and artists. But I work most closely with one writer. It's important for me to work with someone who's good with words.

 Why are you and your writer a good team?

 We trust each other. When we begin a new ad, we each come up with a bunch of dumb ideas. But that's okay, because we keep trying until we have an idea that we both like.

Q **What do you think makes a great ad?**

A A good ad makes people laugh and gets them to remember the product, too.

Q **What is your team's best ad campaign?**

A I think our best ad campaign was for the Liberty Science Center. This is a cool hands-on science museum in New Jersey. My team's job was to spread the news about this exciting place.

Q **How did you come up with exciting ads?**

A To get ideas, the writer and I went to the museum. We played in every exhibit—all 150 of them. Then we went back to the office and brainstormed. We wrote some headlines and drew lots of pictures until we had some great ideas for ads. The good news is that our ad ideas worked! Now the museum is really popular.

Q **When you were a kid, did you ever dream that you would end up in advertising?**

A Not really. But when I was a grocery store clerk, I loved reading cereal boxes. I liked looking at all the different designs. I guess that was a clue.

Max Jerome's Tips for Creating an Ad

1 Know your audience. Think about who will "buy" the product.

2 Know where to put the ad. Think about where most people will see it.

3 Make it unusual. Think about what people will notice about the product.

31

from **Siggy's Spaghetti Works**

by **Peggy Thomson**

illustrated by **Gloria Kamen**

It's a great day for spaghetti. At the Spaghetti Works the floor is shaking. Spaghetti is already rattling down the chutes, and Siggy has flour in his eyebrows, on his elbows, and across his shoes. He calls "Hi!" to the kids at his doorstep. "Welcome!" They've come to see him make spaghetti and pack it into boxes. He will show them from start to finish.

He'll show what to do if it's *their* turn to make tons of it, tons of macaroni, too, noodles, seashells, little bow ties. "And lasagne," says Siggy. "I almost forgot lasagne."

I like spaghetti a lot!

I like a lot of it!

Noodles!

Macaroni!

Lasagne!

Will we eat the homework?

Of course.

"Flour comes first," says Siggy. "It's the big ingredient, and spaghetti-makers need lots. But the great thing is that's ALL they need. Flour plus some water for mixing is the recipe for spaghetti."

Wow! Flour power.

How much flour does it take to make 100 tons of spaghetti? 100 tons of flour and 8 tons just for good measure.

Siggy often telephones farmers to ask, "How are things?" in North Dakota, South Dakota, Minnesota. "Is the weather good? Is the wheat fine?" He's checking on the wheat with the hard, gold kernels—the durum wheat that is ground into flour for spaghetti.

"The tricky part is to get a good mix. Too much water with the flour and *splodge!* the mix is a mess. Too little, and it's a rock." Siggy says, "The mix has to stretch. So when it's pressed through holes in the machine, out come—just what you want—spaghetti strings!"

On Monday Siggy calls the mills. "Hello, hello, help! Our supplies are running low. Please send flour." He asks for semolina, the flour that's ground from durum wheat. Semolina is gritty, like sugar, and spaghetti made from it holds a good shape. It won't go to mush.

"When you make one hundred tons of spaghetti," Siggy says, "it helps to have a factory as big as a city block." A factory like *his*, he means, with railroad tracks to bring the tank cars alongside and hoses to snuffle the flour up into the building.

Siggy asks the mills to send "three tank cars— three hundred tons of flour—please. That should be just enough for now."

Inside, Siggy has silos to keep the flour dry. He has four of them, four stories high, and a lot of machinery, and hundreds of miles of pipes and belts and chutes, and a crew of spaghetti-makers in white hats.

His stairs are plain and steep, but Siggy likes the climb. Two steps at a time, he leads the way up and through the door into his favorite . . .

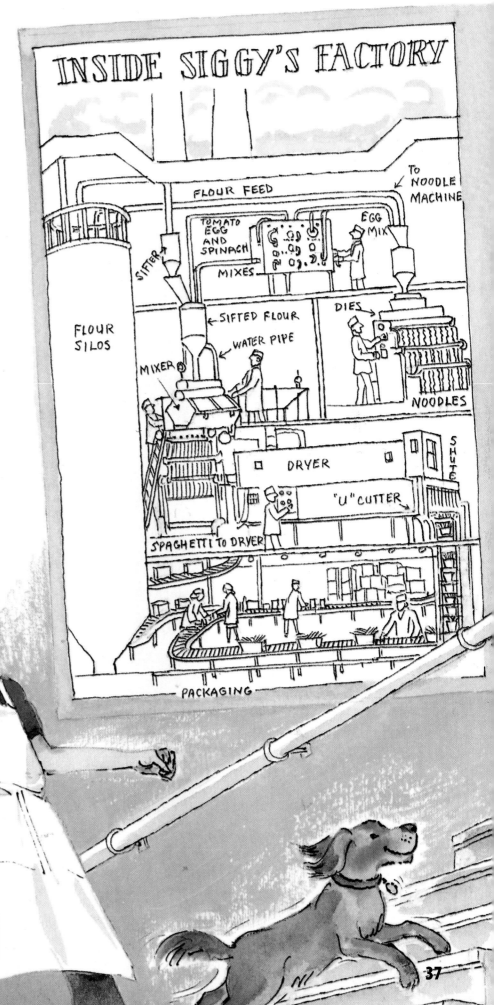

INSIDE SIGGY'S FACTORY

FLOUR FEED

TO NOODLE MACHINE

TOMATO EGG AND SPINACH

EGG MIX

SIFTER

MIXES

FLOUR SILOS

← SIFTED FLOUR

WATER PIPE

MIXER

DIES

NOODLES

DRYER

"U" CUTTER

SHUTE

SPAGHETTI TO DRYER

PACKAGING

37

bright wide-open noisy space where flour rushes through the white pipes, water through the black. This is where spaghetti gets its start, where huge machines (with ladders up their sides) hum and rumble, blinking their lights. "Follow me!" says Siggy, only this time he needs to shout. "To the top, friends, to read the dials and keep watch!

All aboard!

"Now!" Siggy says. "Now is when to check how the rotator blades cut and crumble, mixing the flour and water. Is the mix a wet mess? Is it a rock? This *could* be the surprise bad batch. But . . . it's not! So the fine, stretchy wad of dough down below is pressed upward and out through the rows of little holes.

"Good news! This machine is sending out great rows of spaghetti strings—long and golden white. Perfect!"

Siggy says, "The rods, up above, are moving like clockwork. A whole parade of them. They lift the strings and carry them along—fluttering—into the dryer."

39

"The new, wet spaghetti strings are fine," Siggy says. "They will just hang, drying, in the hot dryer shed until tomorrow."

"And never mind the wait," he says, "because *yesterday's* spaghetti is tumbling out. Hot from the dryer, it's dry and stiff as needles, ready for a ride down the chutes."

If one rod goes off the track, they might all go. And you call in a backhoe to clean up the mess.

DRYER
U's
Siggy's Tip: When dry little U shapes get snipped off—from where the spaghetti hangs over rods—grind them back into flour. Sweep up U's on the floor to sell for pig food.
Who gets the U's?
I love U and U I love U spaghetti.

"No running! is a good rule," says Siggy. "But the spaghetti gets to travel fast. It slides down the chutes from floor to floor, and it rides around on conveyor belts. Bundles of it get weighed and stuffed into skinny boxes with windows. If the boxes pop—more pig food!"

DANGER! LOOK OUT! Dry spaghetti on the floor is slick. It rolls your feet out from under you.

Some old-time spaghetti machines ran on horsepower~ one horse...

or on people power~ to mix the flour and water.

This one batch has cracks... it got too hot in the dryer.

And this batch has dots and spots. It never dried enough. Out with it.

The rest looks just right.

How come Siggy says, no gobbling on the job?

Siggy says, "There's a Help and Rescue call from the kitchens. Testers! Please check the dry spaghetti for quality. Is it tip-top? Tasters! Please taste the cooked spaghetti with care. Does it go to mush or does it stay nicely firm and springy to the teeth?"

It's springy ... my teeth say so.

Some macaroni and noodles have been colored and flavored from the start with squirts from Siggy's pools of spinach and egg and tomato.

Siggy says to watch the boxes. They're on the move, going into cartons. The cartons are going onto skids. And forklifts will deliver them to trucks at the loading dock. Siggy says, "Other boxes at the dock have made the same trip. Some of them are filled with macaroni or noodles or seashells or little bow ties. Some are filled with lasagne."

One carload of flour has become 200,000 boxes of spaghetti, one pound each.

I saw it all!

Siggy says, "Dies—inside the machines—make the different shapes. They're important." He says, "Dies are the heavy metal parts with holes in them, like showerheads, for sending out streams of dough. Spaghetti-makers brag about having good dies and lots of them." Siggy says *his* are terrific. He knows by looking at the holes that "this die is for making spaghetti and that die with the smaller holes is for making spaghetti's extra-skinny sister, spaghettini. The other die with the slots is for lasagne."

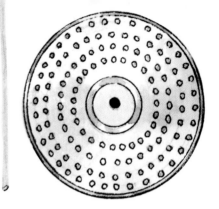

Dies for making SPAGHETTI have small, round holes.

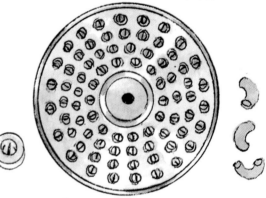

Dies for making MACARONI have round holes with a pin in the holes to make the macaroni hollow. A rotating knife cuts the pieces short. (And a nick in the pin will bend the macaroni to produce ELBOWS.)

I've got dozens of dies to make my shapes.

Another *spaghetti* die, Siggy's favorite, has the spaghetti holes all in a row.

Dies for making LASAGNE have flat slots. The slots turn up at the ends to create lasagne's ruffly edges.

Dies for making ABC's have ABC cut-outs.

The flour-and-water mix for NOODLES has eggs in it. Some noodles go through a die with slits. Others are rolled out flat and cut into strips.

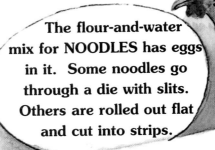

BOW TIES can be cookie-cutter work.

47

Siggy says, "Time flies when there's spaghetti talk. All the mop-up jobs before the bell will have to be fast. There's machinery to oil. Dies to wash. Dies to dry. Labels to lick and stick. Backs to pat, all around, for good work!

"And last of all a fleet of trucks to wave off on trips to faraway cities.

"Good-bye SPAGHETTI, MACARONI,
NOODLES, SEASHELLS, and BOW TIES!
Good-bye, good-bye!"

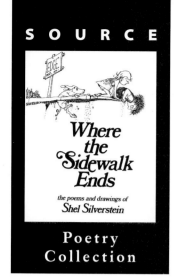

from
Where the Sidewalk Ends

Spaghetti

by *Shel Silverstein*

Spaghetti, spaghetti, all over the place,
Up to my elbows—up to my face,
Over the carpet and under the chairs,
Into the hammock and wound round the stairs,
Filling the bathtub and covering the desk,
Making the sofa a mad mushy mess.

The party is ruined, I'm terribly worried,
The guests have all left (unless they're all buried).
I told them, "Bring presents." I said, "Throw confetti."
I guess they heard wrong
'Cause they all threw spaghetti!

Leaning Fork with Meatball and Spaghetti I

by Claes Oldenburg

This painted aluminum sculpture is almost 11 feet tall.

How to

Design a Cereal Box

Think of all the kinds of cereal you see in the supermarket. There might be four brands of corn flakes alone! Why do you choose one brand and not another? Maybe the design of that cereal box catches your eye. The words and the colors on the box have been carefully chosen so that it "leaps off the shelf."

What is a design? A design is a plan or pattern for something. A cereal box design shows how the pictures and words appear on the box that the cereal comes in.

cereal's name written in large letters

colorful background

photograph makes the cereal look yummy

reasons to buy this cereal

1 Choose a Cereal

As a team, decide what kind of cereal you want to design a box for. To get started, you may want to list your team's favorite cereals. You can choose a real cereal or one that you make up.

TOOLS

- empty cereal box
- construction paper
- paper and pencils
- crayons, colored pencils, paints, scissors

2 Brainstorm Ideas

Bring in different kinds of empty cereal boxes from home. What do you notice about each one?

As a team, brainstorm ideas for the cereal box you'll design.

Tips
- The name should be easy to remember.
- Bright colors and large pictures get attention.

3 Create Your Cereal Box

As a team, decide what you want your cereal box to look like and what words you are going to use on it. Make a drawing that shows where the words and pictures will go. Next, cover an empty cereal box with construction paper. You're ready to add the design. Work together to make the finished cereal box.

4 Present Your Ideas

Cereal companies always test their designs. Your team can, too. Show your cereal box design to your classmates. Tell about the different features on your cereal box and why you chose them. Ask your classmates what they think of your design. Would they buy your cereal? Listen to the other teams' presentations. What good ideas did they have?

If You Are Using a Computer ...

Make your cereal box look professional. Type the words into your computer. Try different sizes and kinds of type. Print out what you've written. Then cut and paste.

THINK

Art directors often decide what the package a product comes in will look like. Why do you think they choose bright colors?

Max Jerome
Art Director ▶

Artists at Work

Discover how a group of carpet weavers save their kingdom. Then join a team of animators as they create a flying carpet.

Learn how a trainer and a special dog create the role of Lassie. Then visit all the people who work for a movie studio.

WORKSHOP 2

Use your imagination to write a catchy slogan.

BE COOL. STAY IN SCHOOL.

SOURCE

The
Legend of the
Persian Carpet
TOMIE dePAOLA
ILLUSTRATED BY CLAIRE EWART

A WHITEBIRD BOOK

Iranian
Folk Tale

58

The Legend of the Persian Carpet

Tomie dePaola

illustrated by Claire Ewart

Many, many years ago, in the land once called Persia, there lived a kind and wise king, who was much loved by his people.

He lived in a white stone palace of many rooms, surrounded by gardens filled with flowers and fruit trees and sparkling fountains. King Balash had everything a man could desire.

But his most prized possession was a large
diamond. This diamond was set on a special pedestal
and was so beautiful and so bright that it filled not only
the room it was in but all the surrounding rooms with a
million rainbows.

King Balash was not a selfish man. He loved and
trusted his people so much that he kept no guards near
the diamond. Every afternoon, when the sun was just
right, and until it set, the king opened the doors of his
palace. Anyone who wished could come to see the walls
of the room painted with the diamond's light.

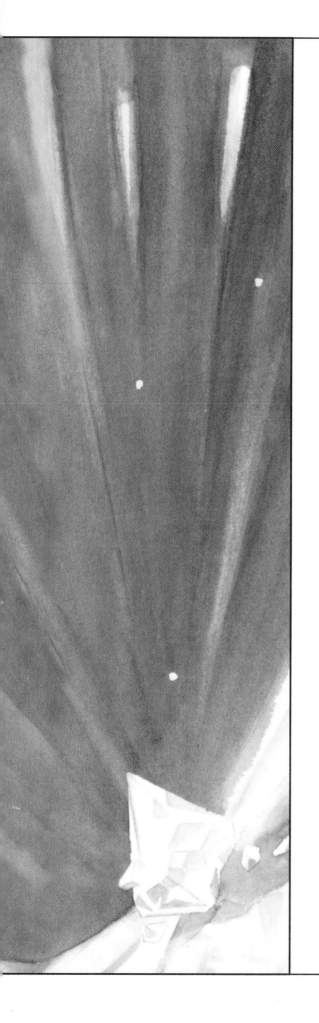

One day at dusk, as the crowds were leaving, a stranger to the kingdom slipped in among the visitors and stole the diamond. Like the wind, the thief raced his horse across the rocky plain toward the desert and the setting sun. But the horse stumbled, the diamond fell from the thief's hand, and it shattered on the rocks. The setting sun shone bloodred on the fragments and reflected a million sunsets into the thief's eyes. He staggered off empty-handed, cursing his luck and rubbing his eyes.

Now it was King Balash's custom to spend the time of the rising sun in the hall of the diamond with its amazing reflections. But instead of a million rainbows, all that greeted the king was the empty pedestal and a room filled with shadows and gloom.

"Call my people!" ordered the king. "I must
tell them of this tragedy. They must help me
find our treasure."

The people set out and soon a small boy named
Payam, who was an apprentice in the Street of
the Weavers, came to the rocky place. The morning
sun shot through the diamond fragments and
dazzled Payam with such a sight that he couldn't

believe his eyes. Off he ran to the palace and was
brought before the king.

"And there, O King," said Payam, "among all the
rocks, is the diamond, broken into a thousand pieces,
sparkling in the sun, reflecting all the colors of the
rainbow on the ground."

"I must see for myself," said the king. "Go
with me."

And when they reached the place, King Balash was
so overwhelmed by the carpet of diamonds that he sat
down and said, "I shall always stay here. I shall never
enter the dark palace again."

"But Sire," cried Payam, "you can't! Who shall rule
the kingdom? Who shall guide the people?"

But King Balash didn't listen. He stared at the
shimmering light, lost in his own thoughts.

The people were all in confusion. Without a leader,

they and their homes could be attacked by any
robber-king from the desert. Their very lives were
in danger.

Payam sat and thought. He called all the other
young apprentices together.

"We must help our king and our people," Payam
told them. "We must make a carpet as miraculous as
the one our king stares at on the rocky plain. We must
all work together."

The apprentices agreed. And so did the master weavers and dyers of silk threads. Everyone set to work.

Payam went to King Balash.

"Please, Sire, come back and sit on the throne for a year and a day," Payam said. "If we cannot fill the room with color and light in that time, then we will accept our fate and live without a king. A year and a day."

It was the least he could do for his people. So King Balash agreed.

Day and night they all worked, spinning, dyeing, weaving on the large rug loom. And in a year and a day, the carpet was finished.

The workers carried the carpet to the palace and into the dark hall where the diamond had rested. With a flourish, they unrolled it before the king.

Suddenly the room was once more filled with the colors of the rainbow. Reds, golds, blues, and greens of the silk carpet glowed on the floor, reflecting color off the walls and the ceiling. Once more, the room was filled with light and King Balash and his people were happy.

And happiest of all were Payam and the other apprentices, for they had not only saved their kingdom, but had made the most beautiful carpet in the world.

High-Tech Carpet

$\mathcal{D}$id you see the movie *Aladdin*? If you did, you know that it's possible to make a carpet fly, creep, and even show feelings— in a movie, at least. Meet the team that used paint, paper, and a computer to make a rug that does much more than lie on a floor!

THE ANIMATOR

Randy Cartwright was the head animator of the team. His job was to do all the drawings of the Magic Carpet. Cartwright had to turn a rug into a movie character. It had to have a winning personality, no less. How did Cartwright do it?

First, Cartwright took a piece of cloth and pretended it was the carpet. He folded the cloth in lots of different ways to see if he could make it look happy, sad, or excited. What a challenge!

Next, Cartwright made some drawings. In one, he drew a fold at the top of the carpet. It looked a little like a head. That was a start. Then, he had the idea of making the tassels seem to be hands and feet. He drew the carpet's "hand" holding its "stomach." Success! The Magic Carpet looked like it was having a good laugh.

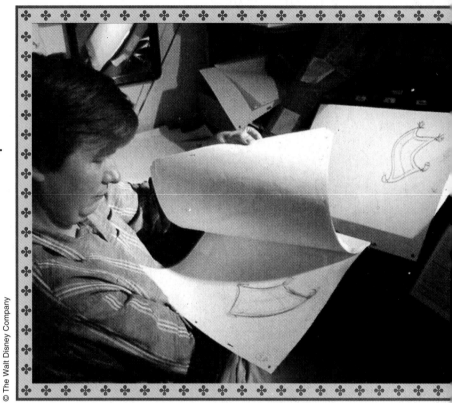

Randy Cartwright flips through drawings so he can see how the carpet looks when it moves.

Believe it or not, a carpet can show many different feelings.

Laughing

Dreamy

Thoughtful

73

Richard Vander Wende made up the Magic Carpet's fancy pattern.

THE ARTIST

Now that the Magic Carpet had a sense of humor, it needed a design, too. So artist Richard Vander Wende created a beautiful one. It included colorful tigers' heads, swords, lamps, and flames.

The next step was to paint the design on every single one of Cartwright's drawings of the carpet. In most cartoons, artists paint everything by hand. Painting Vander Wende's complicated design on hundreds of thousands of drawings would have taken forever. Fortunately, there was another way.

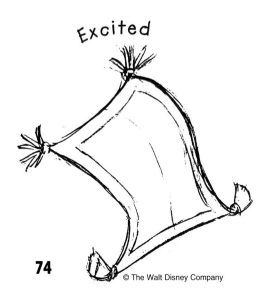

Excited

Curious

Shocked

THE COMPUTER ANIMATOR

Tina Price came to the rescue. She's a computer animator. Her computer has a special program that allows her to create cartoon characters.

First, Price copied Cartwright's black-and-white drawings of the Magic Carpet into her computer. Next, she entered Vander Wende's design into her computer. Then, almost before you could say *Abracadabra*, she "zapped" the colorful design on each computer drawing.

The completed drawings of the Magic Carpet were filmed and added to the other scenes in the movie. By the time the team was finished, Aladdin's Magic Carpet was rolling up with laughter!

© The Walt Disney Company

Tina Price creates the Magic Carpet character on her computer screen.

Me?

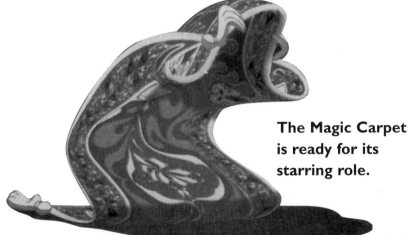

The Magic Carpet is ready for its starring role.

© The Walt Disney Company

75

SOURCE

NATIONAL GEOGRAPHIC
world
Magazine

AWARD
WINNING
Magazine

Stardom Hasn't

Lassie

Spoiled

by McPaul Smith

The Star Stands Tall

★

Coaxed by trainer Bob Weatherwax, Lassie balances on hind legs. Seven dogs have played Lassie in movies, television shows, and exhibitions over the past 50 years. The first was a collie named Pal, trained by Bob's father, Rudd Weatherwax. Lassies have stayed (and heeled and rolled over) in the Weatherwax family ever since.

THE ART OF LYING DOWN
Lassie will assume almost any pose on command, including this one.

White water rushes around the struggling collie. She pulls herself out of the stream, and drags her wet body along the ground into the woods. Soaked, dirty, and exhausted, she collapses. Then the director yells "Cut!" The dog stands up, shakes the water off, and happily accepts a towel, encouraging words, and a bit of steak from a trainer. The trainer's name is Bob Weatherwax; the dog's name is Lassie; and *she* is really a *he*.

Back in 1943 Bob's father, Rudd Weatherwax, trained a male collie named Pal for *Lassie Come Home*, the first Lassie film. It was based on a book by the same name. Seven movies and 19 years' worth of television shows later, Lassie is still the most famous dog in the world. Seven different dogs have played the role, and the eighth is now in training. The Weatherwaxes of Canyon Country, California, have owned and trained all of them. They've raised a lot of collies to find the Lassies.

Why is the right dog so hard to find? Is it brains? Bravery? That beautiful bark? Nope—it's the coloring. Says Bob, "Lassie's coloring is rare. He has a white line, called a blaze, running down his forehead, along with a white fur collar and two white forelegs."

Lassie probably wouldn't win any medals at a dog show. His coloring doesn't conform to the breeders' standards. But the "imperfection" is what makes Lassie Lassie. "The look is trademarked," says Bob. "My father and I have bred thousands of puppies descended from the original Lassie. Only eight males have had the right coloring." Bob thinks male dogs look better on camera. They're bigger, they have fuller coats, and they don't shed as much.

"SICK DOG" is one of hundreds of tricks Bob has taught his star. Lassie first lies still on the ground—and stays limp when picked up. Not much of a trick, you say? Just try it with your dog!

But it's not just the look that makes people love Lassie. He/she is just so smart, brave, and friendly! That's due to the lifetimes Rudd and Bob Weatherwax have spent perfecting their art. Lassie knows about 90 hand signals and verbal commands.

And that's not all. Says Bob: "Remember, these dogs don't just do tricks, they really act. Lassie's mood has to match the mood of the scene. My dad was a real pioneer in dog training. He taught me that my own attitude affects the dog's attitude. If the script calls for the dog to be happy, I'll act happy, and the dog will pick it up."

How does he make sure that Lassie remembers his cues?

HE STARTED IT
That's Pal in the 1943 movie *Lassie Come Home*, with young actor Roddy McDowall. Every dog that has played Lassie in movies and TV since has been descended from Pal.

LASSIE AS DIRECTOR

"Do it again! Do it again!" says Lassie, who seems to want to direct as well as act!

"Repetition, repetition, repetition. And lots of encouragement and petting and positive comments. With patience and skill, you can train any dog."

Not every dog is a great actor, though. "Out of the seven that have played Lassie, four were classic dog-actors," says Bob. "The other three were harder to motivate. I always say, 'It's tough to speed up a slow dog.' But I've learned how to do it."

Bob loves his dogs, and he's pretty sure they love him back. "My dogs spend ten or twelve hours a day getting exercise, attention, and affection," he says. "Most family pets spend a lot of their days alone. Their owners are at work or at school. They'd envy the life that Lassie has. I think it's a great life for a dog."

PICTURE A MOVIE WHERE

THE WARNER BROS. MOVIE WORKS!

Michael Keaton knows what it takes to make a great picture. "As an actor, I have to figure out what makes my character tick, and then show that to the camera. But that's only one piece of the puzzle. It takes a whole team, like the great people at Warner Bros., to put all the pieces of a movie together."

How do they do it?

Dick the Production Designer is responsible for the sets and everything else in front of the camera.

Casting Director Marion helps choose the actors.

CASTING CALL TODAY

SCRIPT

SCRIPT

Cameron is the Scriptwriter. "A good script has characters you care about."

George is the Producer. He raises the money to make the movie and sees to it that everything runs smoothly.

EVERYONE PLAYS A LEADING ROLE.

Joel the Director is in charge of making the movie. "I get the right actors, the right music, the right costumes and the right sets...I hope."

Special Effects expert Patrick loves to build miniatures and make them look like huge landscapes.

STAGE I

Gary heads the Music Department. He helps the director choose a composer to write the score.

Francis oversees the film crew. He creates the photographic look of the picture, its visual style and color.

Willa the Publicist tells magazines, newspapers and TV stations about Warner Bros. films.

Tom is in charge of the Sound Department. He makes sure the dialogue, music, and other effects are mixed together right.

COMMISSARY
STAGE I
POST-PROD.
OFFICE

Dede the Editor explains, "Film is shot in many small sections and from different angles. I put them all together."

MOVIE

How to
Write a
Slogan

Can you think of a short, catchy sentence or phrase that you've heard on the radio or TV? Is there a clever saying about recycling or picking up litter that you say over and over again? It's probably a slogan for a particular product or service.

What is a slogan? A slogan is a phrase or sentence that helps sell a product, a service, or an idea. Slogans are a popular and fun way to advertise. And they're easy to remember!

BE COOL

A public service slogan sells an idea instead of a product.

EVERYONE

EVERYONE FOR BOOKS

·DIANE GOODE·

STAY IN SCHOOL.

Slogans can give an order that grabs your attention.

Slogans can rhyme.

1 What's It About?

With your team, choose a product, service, or idea to create a slogan for. Choose something that you really like or believe in. It could be a favorite food, a new video game, a reminder to recycle, or an upcoming school event. Make a list of your choices. Decide which one you'd like to create a slogan for.

TOOLS

• paper and pencil

2 Brainstorm Ideas

Slogans are everywhere. List some slogans that you and your teammates remember from television and radio ads, posters, or newspapers and magazines. Talk about the slogans with your team. Which ones do you like the most? Why? What makes the slogans easy to remember?

3 Write Your Slogan

Use what you have learned about slogans to create one of your own. These questions may help you.

- What is the best thing about your product, service, or idea?
- What are some fun words that describe the product?

Tips
- Short slogans are easy to remember.
- Rhyming slogans stick in people's minds.
- Using words that start with the same letter can make a slogan sound good.

4 Test Your Slogan

Share your team's slogan with your classmates. Find out if they think your slogan is catchy. Will it encourage them to like your idea, use your service, or buy your product? Listen to the slogans other teams made up. What makes their slogans successful?

If You Are Using a Computer ...

Try printing your slogan in the Banner or Sign format. Use clip art to decorate your work.

THINK

Ad teams use slogans to help people remember products. Which kinds of slogans do you remember best?

Max Jerome
Art Director ▶

At Your Service

Join firefighters as they battle a huge fire in Yellowstone National Park. Then meet another firefighter who raps about fire safety.

Discover how a clever dental team outsmarts a fox with a toothache.

PROJECT

Create an ad campaign for a favorite product or service.

DO YOUR PART AGAIN

89

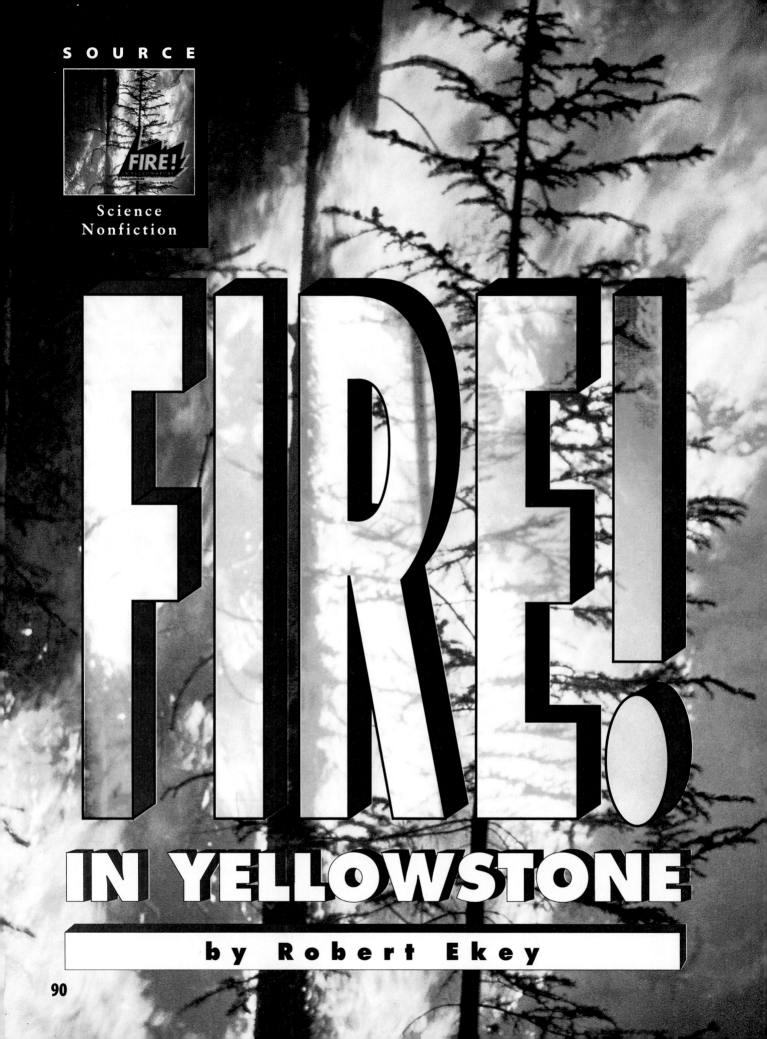

Science
Nonfiction

FIRE!

IN YELLOWSTONE

by Robert Ekey

A bear and cub near Mystic Falls. Most animals escaped the dangerous fires.

In 1988, spring came early in Yellowstone National Park. Snow that usually stays until June melted away under bright, sunny skies. Little rain fell.

The elk, moose, and grizzly bears grazed on an abundant supply of grass and other plants. Old Faithful geyser gushed as tourists snapped photographs. Yellowstone did not appear to be in a drought, but the forest was dry.

In June, a bolt of lightning struck a tree and started a small forest fire. Soon, lightning struck in other areas and started more fires in Yellowstone and on nearby forest lands. Each fire sent up a small column of smoke.

At first, park rangers allowed the fires to burn. Rangers had learned that fire has always been a vital part of the forest ecology, or the relationship between living things and their surroundings. Fire clears away old trees to make room for new plants and trees. Fires are as important to the growth of the forest as sunshine and rain.

This was not the first time Yellowstone had seen fires. Every year lightning starts fires. In fact, centuries ago, Native Americans used to light fires to drive game to hunters and to improve wildlife habitats.

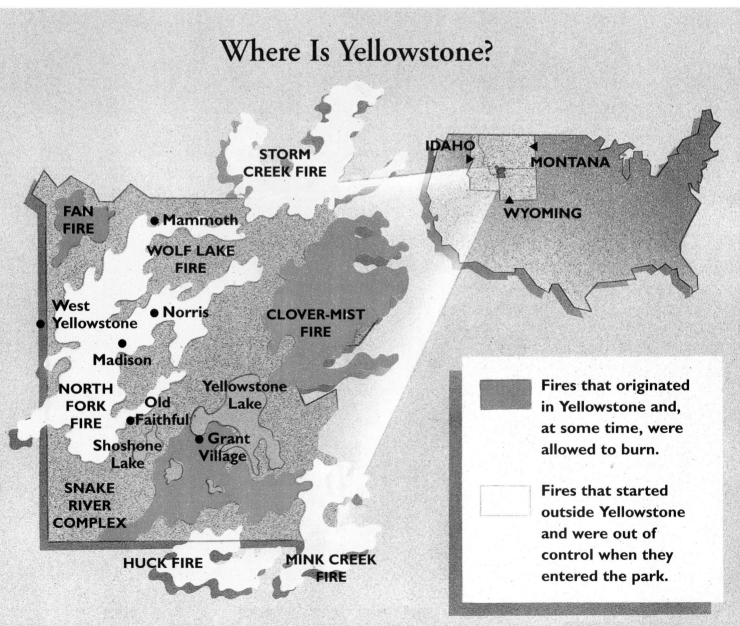

Where Is Yellowstone?

STORM CREEK FIRE

IDAHO
MONTANA
WYOMING

FAN FIRE

● Mammoth

WOLF LAKE FIRE

West Yellowstone

● Norris

CLOVER-MIST FIRE

Madison

NORTH FORK FIRE

Old Faithful

Yellowstone Lake

Shoshone Lake

● Grant Village

SNAKE RIVER COMPLEX

HUCK FIRE

MINK CREEK FIRE

Fires that originated in Yellowstone and, at some time, were allowed to burn.

Fires that started outside Yellowstone and were out of control when they entered the park.

Firefighter Jill Jayne studies the fire as it moves through the treetops.

Most of the fires that start go out by themselves. Those that burn usually burn only a few acres. But 1988 was a different year. The heat of the summer and lack of rain left the forest very dry.

The fires in and near Yellowstone grew bigger. A careless woodcutter started another fire.

By the end of July, fires were close to buildings, and tourists moved from their campsites. Rangers decided they should try to put out all fires.

Most states sent firefighters to Yellowstone to battle the blazes. These young men and women fought hard to control the fires.

Bison calm in the midst of fires. Elk and moose often entered burnt areas to eat.

But by August, the fires had continued to spread. No rain fell, and winds fanned the flames. Some days, the wind blew at gale force, spreading the fires over thousands of acres. Flames 200 feet tall swept through the forest faster than people can walk.

As the fires burned in the forest, the elk, bison, and other animals could easily escape the flames. Sometimes they were seen calmly grazing near the fires.

Many people who live near Yellowstone asked why rangers did not put out the fires. By then, the fires were too big. The worst drought in a century had left the forest too dry. The fires could not be stopped.

Clover-Mist fire at the foot of Pilot Peak. It was a dangerous fire but beautiful at night.

Firefighting, modern and traditional: Firefighters used planes to take infrared maps of the land. They flew air tankers carrying water and chemicals that retard flames. They called in fire trucks from many stations. But to do this grueling work, they also had to use shovels, mules, and Pulaskis (a combination hoe and axe).

Thousands of firefighters were called to help, including soldiers from the U.S. Army and Marines. They used helicopters and airplanes to drop millions of gallons of water and chemicals on the fires. Firefighters used special tools to dig trails in the forest, in an attempt to stop the flames.

Every morning, smoke blanketed Yellowstone. Every afternoon, high winds blew, sending burning embers flying high in the sky. When the embers landed, they started more fires. Thousands of acres were on fire, and huge smoke columns filled the sky.

In early September—when the smoke column showed the fire was moving closer—tourists were still visiting Old Faithful. Firefighters sprayed buildings with water to keep them from burning.

Suddenly, the fire crested the ridge near Old Faithful! Rangers ordered tourists to leave quickly. A fierce firestorm swept across the parking lot near the old hotel there. It sent embers the size of golf balls skipping across the pavement.

The firestorm surprised firefighters. Many raced to help protect buildings and put out small fires started by the embers.

The fire at Old Faithful burned many trees and a few small cabins. But the larger buildings were saved, including the big old log hotel called the Old Faithful Inn. The fire seemed to pass as quickly as it came.

The next week, it started to rain and snow. It was the first rain in the park in weeks. The rain did what ten thousand firefighters could not do—it started to put the fires out.

The North Fork fire consumes one of the buildings of the Old Faithful complex. Flames devoured 16 buildings in all.

Inset: Firefighters wet the roof of the Norris Museum to protect it from embers.

By mid-September, nearly one million acres had burned in Yellowstone and 400 thousand in nearby forests. The area burned is the same size as the state of Delaware, but still less than half of the park was burned.

During the fires, many people argued that Yellowstone officials should have tried to put the fires out sooner. The officials answered that they could not have forecast the extreme drought conditions.

Only nature could stop what it started with the drought. "This is Mother Nature at work," one park ranger said. In the future, rangers decided, some fires will still be allowed to burn, but they will be watched more closely.

Left: Grass sprouts from the charred earth.

Middle: By spring, flowers are blooming and spreading through the forest.

Right: The heat of the fire caused lodgepole pine seeds to pop from their cones. They then rooted in the fertile ash and are now becoming a new forest.

Snow covered Yellowstone early in October. Early the next spring, the snow melted, providing water for the seeds and roots that had survived underground.

Where meadows had been burned, wildflowers bloomed in the spring and summer. In the forested areas, thousands of lodgepole pine seedlings sprouted as the forest was born again. None of the geysers was changed by the fire.

While fire forced some animals to move from the forest, it also provided new food sources for other wildlife. Biologists say that animals and plants adapt to fire. For some animals, fire even makes life easier.

Now, much rain has fallen, and the drought is over. Elk and bison graze on the new wildflowers and grasses. Birds sing in the trees. And tourists return to take pictures of the animals, the geysers, and the fresh young plants growing from the forest floor.

The Life Cycle of a Lodgepole Forest

| Mature Forest | Fire | 0–60 Years |

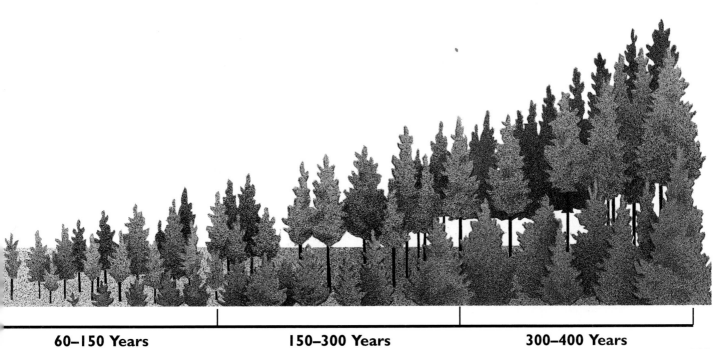

60–150 Years　　　**150–300 Years**　　　**300–400 Years**

SMOKE JUMPER

Smoke jumper Margarita Phillips is well suited to fight a fire. Smoke jumpers put together and repair their own gear—except for their boots and helmets. The equipment Phillips jumps with weighs 85 pounds.

JUMPSUIT The heavily padded jumpsuit is made of the same material as bulletproof vests worn by police officers. Smoke jumpers wear fire-resistant clothing underneath.

RESERVE CHUTE If the main parachute does not open, the reserve chute gets pulled into service.

PACK-OUT BAG Tucked away in a jumpsuit, this bag is empty at first. Most fire fighting equipment is dropped to the ground in a separate container. Once a fire is out, a smoke jumper puts the equipment in the bag so it can be carried out.

MAIN PARACHUTE Within five seconds of leaving the plane, a smoke jumper's parachute opens. It is carried inside a backpack.

STATIC LINE A yellow nylon strap connects the main parachute to a cable inside the plane. The strap helps pull open the chute, which then disconnects.

HELMET A motorcycle helmet has a protective metal face guard.

LEG POCKETS Inside go long johns and the "bird's nest"—looped nylon strap (shown on top of the pack-out bag) that smoke jumpers use to descend if they land in a tree. Also inside are signal streamers for communicating with the pilot from the ground.

CROSSCUT SAW Dropped to the ground in a cargo box, the saw is used to clear timber and branches from a fire line. Here the saw is bent over the pack-out bag and its teeth are covered.

Firefighter Raps It Up!

SOURCE

SCHOLASTIC NEWS®

News Magazine

AWARD WINNING

Magazine

Firefighter Johnny Ruiz has a cool new way to teach fire safety tips to kids. He raps them. Here is one of Ruiz's raps.

Smoke Detectors

A **smoke detector**
saves lives and property.

But like a brand new toy,
it won't work
without a **battery**.

A marvelous machine,
it should be **tested**.

It's just like a firefighter
who is **never rested**.

Firefighters know
what detectors **can do**.

That's why I **rap**
this message to you.

A detector's on duty,
day and night.

Will it keep you **safe**?
It just might!

Doctor De Soto

by WILLIAM STEIG

Doctor De Soto, the dentist, did very good
work, so he had no end of patients. Those close to his
own size—moles, chipmunks, et cetera—sat in the regular
dentist's chair.

Larger animals sat on the floor, while Doctor De Soto
stood on a ladder.

For extra-large animals, he had a special room. There Doctor De Soto was hoisted up to the patient's mouth by his assistant, who also happened to be his wife.

Doctor De Soto was especially popular with the big animals. He was able to work inside their mouths, wearing rubbers to keep his feet dry; and his fingers were so delicate, and his drill so dainty, they could hardly feel any pain.

Being a mouse, he refused to treat animals dangerous to mice, and it said so on his sign. When the doorbell rang, he and his wife would look out the window. They wouldn't admit even the most timid-looking cat.

One day, when they looked out, they saw a well-dressed fox with a flannel bandage around his jaw.

"I cannot treat you, sir!" Doctor De Soto shouted. "Sir! Haven't you read my sign?"

"Please!" the fox wailed. "Have mercy, I'm suffering!" And he wept so bitterly it was pitiful to see.

"Just a moment," said Doctor De Soto. "That poor fox," he whispered to his wife. "What shall we do?"

"Let's risk it," said Mrs. De Soto. She pressed the buzzer and let the fox in.

He was up the stairs in a flash. "Bless your little hearts," he cried, falling to his knees. "I beg you, *do* something! My tooth is killing me."

"Sit on the floor, sir," said Doctor De Soto, "and remove the bandage, please."

Doctor De Soto climbed up the ladder and bravely entered the fox's mouth. "Ooo-wow!" he gasped. The fox had a rotten bicuspid and unusually bad breath.

"This tooth will have to come out," Doctor De Soto announced. "But we can make you a new one."

"Just stop the pain," whimpered the fox, wiping some tears away.

Despite his misery, he realized he had a tasty little morsel in his mouth, and his jaw began to quiver. "Keep open!" yelled Doctor De Soto. "Wide open!" yelled his wife.

"I'm giving you gas now," said Doctor De Soto. "You won't feel a thing when I yank that tooth."

Soon the fox was in dreamland. "M-m-m, yummy," he mumbled. "How I love them raw . . . with just a pinch of salt, and a . . . dry . . . white wine."

They could guess what he was dreaming about. Mrs. De Soto handed her husband a pole to keep the fox's mouth open.

Doctor De Soto fastened his extractor to the bad tooth. Then he and his wife began turning the winch. Finally, with a sucking sound, the tooth popped out and hung swaying in the air.

"I'm bleeding!" the fox yelped when he came to.

Doctor De Soto ran up the ladder and stuffed some gauze in the hole. "The worst is over," he said. "I'll have your new tooth ready tomorrow. Be here at eleven sharp."

The fox, still woozy, said goodbye and left. On his way home, he wondered if it would be shabby of him to eat the De Sotos when the job was done.

After office hours, Mrs. De Soto molded a tooth of pure gold and polished it. "Raw with salt, indeed," muttered Doctor De Soto. "How foolish to trust a fox!"

"He didn't know what he was saying," said Mrs. De Soto. "Why should he harm us? We're helping him."

"Because he's a fox!" said Doctor De Soto. "They're wicked, wicked creatures."

That night the De Sotos lay awake worrying. "Should we let him in tomorrow?" Mrs. De Soto wondered.

"Once I start a job," said the dentist firmly, "I finish it. My father was the same way."

"But we must do something to protect ourselves," said his wife. They talked and talked until they formed a plan. "I think it will work," said Doctor De Soto. A minute later he was snoring.

The next morning, promptly at eleven, a very cheerful fox turned up. He was feeling not a particle of pain.

When Doctor De Soto got into his mouth, he snapped it shut for a moment, then opened wide and laughed. "Just a joke!" he chortled.

"Be serious," said the dentist sharply. "We have work to do." His wife was lugging the heavy tooth up the ladder.

"Oh, I love it!" exclaimed the fox. "It's just beautiful."

Doctor De Soto set the gold tooth in its socket and hooked it up to the teeth on both sides.

The fox caressed the new tooth with his tongue.

"My, it feels good," he thought. "I really shouldn't eat them. On the other hand, how can I resist?"

"We're not finished," said Doctor De Soto, holding up a large jug. "I have here a remarkable preparation developed only recently by my wife and me. With just one application, you can be rid of toothaches forever. How would you like to be the first one to receive this unique treatment?"

"I certainly would!" the fox declared. "I'd be honored." He hated any kind of personal pain.

"You will never have to see us again," said Doctor De Soto.

"*No one* will see you again," said the fox to himself. He had definitely made up his mind to eat them—with the help of his brand-new tooth.

Doctor De Soto stepped into the fox's mouth with a bucket of secret formula and proceeded to paint each tooth. He hummed as he worked. Mrs. De Soto stood by on the ladder, pointing out spots he had missed. The fox looked very happy.

When the dentist was done, he stepped out. "Now close your jaws tight," he said, "and keep them closed for a full minute." The fox did as he was told. Then he tried to open his mouth—but his teeth were stuck together!

"Ah, excuse me, I should have mentioned," said Doctor De Soto, "you won't be able to open your mouth for a day or two. The secret formula must first permeate the dentine. But don't worry. No pain ever again!"

The fox was stunned. He stared at Doctor De Soto, then at his wife. They smiled, and waited. All he could do was say, "Frank oo berry mush" through his clenched teeth, and get up and leave. He tried to do so with dignity.

Then he stumbled down the stairs in a daze.

Doctor De Soto and his assistant had outfoxed the fox. They kissed each other and took the rest of the day off.

How to

Create an Ad Campaign

Work with **your** *team* to **plan** all kinds of **ads.**

How does a company tell the world about a new product or service? One way is to create an advertising, or ad, campaign. An ad campaign can include TV and radio commercials, ads in magazines, billboards, bumper stickers, and even T-shirts! Who thinks of all these different kinds of ads? A special team of writers and artists at an ad agency does. Each team member brings special skills and knowledge to an ad campaign.

Stay
on

1 Research a Product

With your team, choose a product, a service, or a fun place to go—like a park or museum—for your ad campaign. Pick something that team members like and know about. Next, ask yourselves, "What's so great about this product?" Brainstorm and list reasons that people should use it.

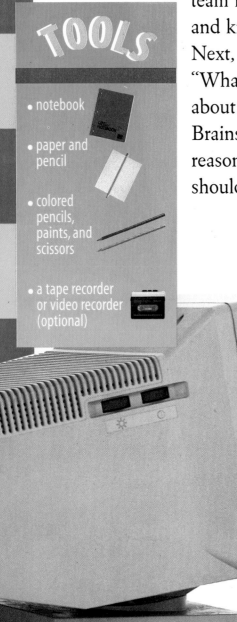

TOOLS

- notebook
- paper and pencil
- colored pencils, paints, and scissors
- a tape recorder or video recorder (optional)

Think of things that make your product better than others of its kind. Do some market research. Ask people you know what they like about your product. This will help you decide how to advertise it.

Your team may want to create a public-service ad campaign. Public-service ads present useful information. They may tell about staying healthy and safe, taking care of nature, or even recycling.

2 Do Your Part

As a group, decide which kinds of ads to create for your campaign. Then, as a team, decide what each member will do. The jobs might include: writing magazine and newspaper ads; creating radio and TV scripts; making up jingles or songs about the product; thinking of a slogan; and designing posters, buttons, billboards, hats, or T-shirts.

Before you begin the ad campaign, look at and listen to lots of ads to get ideas. Share what you find with your team.

How Am I Doing?

Before your team begins to create an ad campaign, ask yourselves these questions.

- Have we chosen a product that all team members agree on?

- Have we brainstormed ideas about why people would want to buy this product?

- Have we asked others what they think about this product?

Tip Keep your ads simple. The fewer the words, the easier they will be to remember.

STAY ON TRACK

STAY ★ TRACK

↑ I like the hurdle idea.

This one works better in black and white. ↓

Try using different colors. ↓

STAY ON TRACK

STAY ON TRACK

Start the Campaign

Create ads for your campaign. Make them fun and lively. If you are making a radio or TV commercial, you might want to tape it. As a team, look at all the ads you created. Are they exciting and colorful? Will the ads make people want to buy the product? Make any changes your group decides on. Now your campaign is ready to go.

Stay on Track

Snazzy Sneakers

1st Place

4 Present Your Ads

As a team, present your ads to the class. Team members can show the parts of the campaign they worked on. Ask your classmates how they feel about your product. Look at other teams' presentations.

What good ideas did they have? What kinds of products and ads did they choose? Discuss how working together helped create successful ad campaigns.

If You Are Using a Computer...

Use your computer to design magazine and newspaper ads with the Sign format. Try different kinds and sizes of type and clip art, too. Then print out your exciting new ads. You can also type your advertising slogans in the Banner format to print out and hang up in the classroom.

CONGRATULATIONS

Now you know what it's like to get a job done—and to work on a team. Look around you. What other jobs are done by teams?

Max Jerome
Art Director ▶

Glossary

ap·pren·tic·es
(ə pren′ti siz) *noun*
People who work with and learn from a more experienced person.
▲ **apprentice**

batch (bach) *noun*
A group of things made or put together at the same time. I made a *batch* of biscuits.

bi·cus·pid
(bī kus′pid) *noun*
A tooth with two points on its top.

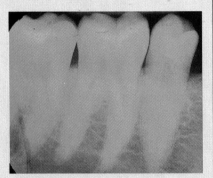
bicuspid

blaz·es
(blā′ziz) *noun*
Burning fires or flames.
▲ **blaze**

chutes
(sho͞ots) *noun*
Long tubes or passages through which things can be dropped. The worker dropped the letters into the mail *chutes*. ▲ **chute**

Word History

The word **chute** comes from an old French word that means "to fall." Objects that are put into a chute fall or drop into another area.

clock·work
(klok′wûrk′) *noun*
Something that moves at a steady rate or regular pace, like the insides of a clock.

col·umns
(kol′əmz) *noun*
Things having the shape or form of long, thin, upright structures that support a building. *Columns* of smoke rose from the burning forest.
▲ **column**

com·plained
(kəm plānd′) *verb*
Said that something was unpleasant or wrong. We *complained* that the noise was too loud.
▲ **complain**

con·ceit·ed
(kən sēt′ əd) *adjective*
Having too high an opinion of oneself. She is so *conceited* that she couldn't believe she wasn't chosen to be in the play.

conveyor belt

con•vey•or belts
(kən vā′er belts′) *noun*
Continuous belts that
are used to carry things
from one place to
another. At the super-
market, the *conveyor
belts* move groceries to
the cash registers.
▲ **conveyor belt**

Word History

The **conveyor belt** was
invented around 1905
to help move things in
factories. The word
conveyor comes from the
word *convey*. *Convey*
means to carry or to take
from one place to another.

cues (kyo͞oz) *noun*
Signals that tell someone
when to do something.
▲ **cue**

den•tine
(den′tēn) *noun*
The hard, thick material
that makes up most of a
tooth. It is inside the
tooth.

de•sign (di zīn′) *verb*
To arrange the parts,
colors, or patterns of
something. Did you
design the patterns on
this rug?

di•a•logue (dī′ə log)
noun
Conversation between
characters in a movie,
play, or any other
performance.

di•als (dī′əlz) *noun*
The faces of instruments,
clocks, or water meters.
Dials have numbers or
letters and a pointer that
points to these markings.
Dials give information.
▲ **dial**

di•rec•tor (də rek′ tər)
noun
The person in charge of
making a movie, a play,
or a television or radio
show.

drought (drout) *noun*
A long period of dry
weather.

dy•ers (dī′erz) *noun*
People who change the
color of fabric using
dye—a substance that
alters the color of
something. ▲ **dyer**

em•bers
(em′berz) *noun*
Small pieces of burned
wood that are still hot
and glowing in the ashes
of a fire. ▲ **ember**

a	add	o͞o	took	ə =
ā	ace	o͞o	pool	a in *above*
â	care	u	up	e in *sicken*
ä	palm	û	burn	i in *possible*
e	end	yo͞o	fuse	o in *melon*
ē	equal	oi	oil	u in *circus*
i	it	ou	pout	
ī	ice	ng	ring	
o	odd	th	thin	
ō	open	ŧh	this	
ô	order	zh	vision	

Glossary

ex·trac·tor
(ik strak′tər) *noun*
A machine that pulls something out with great force. We used an *extractor* to take the water out of the wet rug.

fire·storm
(fīər′stôrm′) *noun*
A giant fire that moves very quickly–like a storm. Firestorms are often pushed by strong winds.

fork·lifts (fôrk′lifts′)
noun
Small vehicles with a fork-shaped tool on the front. *Forklifts* are used to lift heavy objects.
▲ **forklift**

forklift

gasped (gaspt) *verb*
Took in a quick breath of air because of a surprise or shock. She *gasped* with surprise when she received the award.
▲ **gasp**

gauze (gôz) *noun*
A light, thin cloth that is often used for bandages.

large (lärj) *adjective*
Very big.

Thesaurus

large

huge
giant
gigantic
enormous

light·ning
(līt′ning) *noun*
A sudden flash of light in the sky caused by a buildup of electricity in the air.

Fact File

• At any one time, there are 1,800 thunderstorms happening all over the world. That means **lightning** is striking the earth 100 times every second.

• It is said that lightning never strikes the same place more than once. But some buildings—like the Empire State Building in New York City—have been struck again and again.

loom (lo͞om) *noun*
A machine for weaving thread or yarn into cloth.

loom

mu·ti·ny
(myo͞o′ tə nē) *noun*
An uprising; a rebellion or fight against the way things are.

perked (pûrkt) *verb*
Became lively or felt happy again. The sick boy *perked* up after he watched the funny cartoon. ▲ **perk**

role (rōl) *noun*
A part played by an actor or other performer.

scene (sēn) *noun*
One section or situation in a movie, a play, or a television show. Everyone cried during the sad *scene* at the hospital.

script (skript) *noun*
The written text telling actors their lines in a movie, play, or any show.

sets (sets) *noun*
Places built to be the scenes of action in a movie, a play, or other show. Many people worked on building the *sets* for the spaceship for our time travel show.
▲ **set**

si•los (sī′lōz) *noun*
Huge towers that are used for storing grains, such as wheat or corn.
▲ **silo**

smoke (smōk) *noun*
A cloud or mist that rises from something that is burning. The *smoke* from our campfire got in our eyes.

smoke

spin•ning (spin′ing) *verb*
Making long, thin pieces of fiber into yarn or thread. The worker is *spinning* thread from pieces of cotton.
▲ **spin**

tooth•aches (tōōth′āks′) *noun*
Pains in or near teeth.
▲ **toothache**

weav•ers (wē′vərz) *noun*
Workers who make cloth or rugs on a loom by passing threads or yarn over and under in a crisscross pattern.
▲ **weaver**

yank (yangk) *verb*
To give a sudden, strong pull. I *yank* the leash when my dog runs toward the street.

a	add	ŏŏ	took	ə =
ā	ace	ōō	pool	a in *above*
â	care	u	up	e in *sicken*
ä	palm	û	burn	i in *possible*
e	end	yōō	fuse	o in *melon*
ē	equal	oi	oil	u in *circus*
i	it	ou	pout	
ī	ice	ng	ring	
o	odd	th	thin	
ō	open	th	this	
ô	order	zh	vision	

Authors & Illustrators

Tomie dePaola *pages 58–71*

Tomie dePaola says, "It's a dream of mine that one of my books . . . will touch the heart of some individual child and change that child's life for the better." He has written and illustrated nearly 200 books for children. *The Legend of the Persian Carpet* is the first that he has not illustrated himself. He says, "I do a lot of writing in my head first, just thinking the story through." Then he revises many times until he gets a final draft. Although he has written all kinds of books, dePaola is especially fond of folk tales.

Claire Ewart *pages 58–71*

Artist Claire Ewart looked at hundreds of Persian carpets before she illustrated *The Legend of the Persian Carpet*. Creating pictures for a book like this takes a lot of research. It also takes imagination. In the end, she was able to show how people lived long ago in Persia. She also captured the warmth and beauty of their wonderful carpets.

Jeanne Modesitt *pages 10–27*

How does Jeanne Modesitt get ideas for her new stories? She sees her ideas in her head. For her, story writing is like watching a short animated film. She likes to make kids laugh with her words and help them dream and hope. She says, "It's a wonderful job, writing for kids; I wouldn't change it for anything."

Shel Silverstein *page 50*

When Shel Silverstein was growing up, he wanted to be a baseball player. Because he couldn't play ball, he began to draw and write instead. He feels lucky not to have found any writers to imitate, because it helped him develop his own special style early in his career.

William Steig

pages 106–121
Author/illustrator William Steig wrote his first book for children when he was 61 years old. Since then, he has written many books that have become kid's favorites. In his stories, anything can happen— and quite often does.

"Writing is fun. If you write, you discover things about yourself in the process."

Peggy Thomson *pages 32–49*

Peggy Thomson's travels have taken her to China—many years after Marco Polo's visit. She began her career as a magazine writer. Since then, she has written hundreds of magazine and newspaper articles. Her other children's books include the award-winning *Auks, Rocks & the Odd Dinosaur*.

Books &

More by William Steig

Brave Irene
Irene's mother is making a dress for the Duchess to wear at a big party. Then Irene's mother gets sick, and a huge snowstorm blocks the roads. Without Irene's help the Duchess won't get her dress. Can one little girl really take care of everything?

Dr. De Soto in Africa
This dedicated dentist faces a new challenge when he meets an elephant with a toothache.

Sylvester and the Magic Pebble
Sylvester the donkey discovers it's not always a good thing when wishes come true!

The Giraffe, the Pelly, and Me
by Roald Dahl
In this funny fantasy, a boy, a giraffe, and a pelican run a window-washing business.

Fat Chance, Claude!
by Joan Lowery Nixon
illustrated by Tracey Campbell
Shirley goes off to find gold and meets up with Claude. They help each other along the way—until they both spot gold on the same site!

The Patchwork Quilt
by Valerie Flournoy
illustrated by Jerry Pinkney
Tanya watches and listens as Grandma pieces together a patchwork quilt. When Grandma can no longer work on the quilt, Tanya and the rest of her family decide to finish the job.

Bill Hanna & Joe Barbera: Yabba-Dabba-Do!
by Keith Elliot Greenberg
Find out how the creators of *Yogi Bear* and other popular cartoon shows work together.

Corn Belt Harvest
by Raymond Bial
This colorful photo essay shows the work that goes into raising corn.

Cowboys
by Charles Sullivan
This unusual book combines art with original poems. The result? A special look at how cowboys of long ago did their jobs.

xMedia

Videos

Ailey Dancers: The Alvin Ailey American Dance Theater
Kultar

See Alvin Ailey's dance troupe in this video that records some of their dances. (90 minutes)

Almost Partners
Public Media

This *WonderWorks* mystery involves a detective and his young "assistant," Molly. How did a valuable vase find its way to Molly's grandfather's house? (55 minutes)

Piggy Banks to Money Markets: A Kid's Video Guide to Dollars and Sense
Kidviz

In this video, kids talk about money management. (30 minutes)

Software

Granny Applebee's Cookie Factory
Micrograms
(Apple)

Can you follow recipes? Can you fix machines? This challenging game allows you to try many jobs and solve lots of problems.

Superprint II
Scholastic Inc.
(Apple, IBM, Macintosh)

This program can help you make great-looking posters, greeting cards, calendars, ads, and more.

Magazines

3-2-1 Contact
Children's Television Workshop

This magazine is full of information about how people use technology and science in all kinds of jobs.

A Place to Write

Business Kids
301 Almeric Avenue
Suite 330
Coral Gables, FL 33134

What kinds of jobs can kids do? *Business Kids* can help you team up with other kids who share your interest in running a business.

Acknowledgments

Grateful acknowledgment is made to the following sources for permission to reprint from previously published material. The publisher has made diligent efforts to trace the ownership of all copyrighted material in this volume and believes that all necessary permissions have been secured. If any errors or omissions have inadvertently been made, proper corrections will gladly be made in future editions.

Cover: Picture from DOCTOR DE SOTO by William Steig. Copyright © 1982 by William Steig. Reprinted by permission of Farrar, Straus, & Giroux, Inc.

Interior: "The Story of Z" from THE STORY OF Z by Jean Modesitt, illustrated by Lonni Sue Johnson. Text copyright © 1990 by Jeanne Modesitt. Illustrations copyright © 1990 by Lonni Sue Johnson. Reprinted with permission of Simon and Schuster Books for Young Readers, Simon & Schuster Children's Publishing Division.

"The Bug Zoo" poster is used by the kind permission of the Liberty Science Center, Jersey City, NJ.

Excerpt and cover from SIGGY'S SPAGHETTI WORKS by Peggy Thomson, illustrated by Gloria Kamen. Text copyright © 1993 by Peggy Thomson. Illustrations copyright © 1993 by Gloria Kamen. Reprinted by permission of Tambourine Books, a division of William Morrow & Company, Inc.

"Spaghetti" and cover from WHERE THE SIDEWALK ENDS by Shel Silverstein. Copyright © 1974 by Evil Eye Music, Inc. Reprinted by permission of HarperCollins Publishers.

"The Legend of the Persian Carpet" from THE LEGEND OF THE PERSIAN CARPET by Tomie dePaola, illustrated by Claire Ewart. Text copyright © 1993 by Tomie dePaola, illustrations copyright © 1993 by Claire Ewart. Reprinted by permission of G. P. Putnam's Sons.

"Disney" signature logo, illustration, and photos for "High Tech Carpet" copyright © The Walt Disney Company.

"Stardom Hasn't Spoiled Lassie" from National Geographic WORLD, copyright © September 1993 National Geographic Society. Reprinted by permission of National Geographic WORLD.

"Picture a Movie" and Time Warner logo appear by permission of Time Warner.

"Books for Everyone" bookmark illustrated by Diane Goode. Copyright © 1994 by Scholastic Inc. Used by permission.

"Fire! In Yellowstone" from FIRE! IN YELLOWSTONE by Robert Ekey. Text copyright © 1990 by Falcon Press Publishing Co., Inc. Format copyright © 1990 by Gareth Stevens, Inc. Used by permission of Gareth Stevens, Inc., Milwaukee, WI.

"Smoke Jumper" from National Geographic WORLD, copyright © August 1994 National Geographic Society. Reprinted by permission of National Geographic WORLD, the official magazine for Junior Members of the National Geographic Society.

"Smoke Detectors" by Johnny Ruiz. Copyright © 1992 by Johnny Ruiz. Reprinted by permission of the author.

Text, illustrations, and cover from DOCTOR DE SOTO by William Steig. Copyright © 1982 by William Steig. Reprinted by permission of Farrar, Straus & Giroux, Inc.

Cover from ALVIN AILEY by Andrea Davis Pinkney, illustrated by Brian Pinkney. Illustration copyright © 1993 by Brian Pinkney. Published by Hyperion Books for Children.

Cover from THE BOXCAR CHILDREN: THE PIZZA MYSTERY created by Gertrude Chandler Warner, illustrated by Charles Tang. Illustration copyright © 1993 by Albert Whitman & Company. Published by Albert Whitman & Company. THE BOXCAR CHILDREN is a registered trademark of Albert Whitman & Co.

Cover from FINDING THE TITANIC by Robert D. Ballard, illustrated by Ken Marschall. Illustration copyright © 1993 by Madison Press Limited. Published by Madison Press Limited.

Cover from MIRETTE ON THE HIGH WIRE by Emily Arnold McCully. Illustration copyright © 1992 by Emily Arnold McCully. Published by The Putnam & Grosset Book Group.

Photography and Illustration Credits

Photos: © John Lei for Scholastic Inc. all Tool Box items unless otherwise noted. p. 2 all: © John Lei for Scholastic Inc. pp. 2-3 background: © Merry Alpern for Scholastic Inc. p. 3 bc: © John Lei for Scholastic Inc. pp. 4-6: © Ana Esperanza Nance. p. 28: © Merry Alpern for Scholastic Inc. p. 29: © John Lei for Scholastic Inc. p. 30 cr: © Merry Alpern for Scholastic Inc; bl: © John Lei for Scholastic Inc. p. 31 cr: © John Lei for Scholastic Inc. p. 51 br: © Ken Karp for Scholastic Inc.; c: © Claes Oldenburg/The Pace Gallery. p. 52 bc: © Richard Lee for Scholastic Inc.; br: © David S. Waitz for Scholastic Inc. p. 53 c: © John Lei for Scholastic Inc. pp. 54-55: © John Lei for Scholastic Inc. p. 54-55 c: © Stanley Bach for Scholastic Inc. pp. 76-79 © Daniel R. Westergren/National Geographic Society Image Collection. p. 80: © 1943 Turner Entertainment Co. p. 81: © Bob Greene/Paramount Pictures. pp. 86-87 bc: © Stanley Bach for Scholastic Inc. p. 87 br: © John Lei for Scholastic Inc. p. 90 c: © Bob Zellar. p. 91 tc: © Bob Zellar. p. 93 cr: © Bob Zellar. p. 94 woods on fire: © Bob Zellar. p. 95 tc: © Larry Mayer. p. 96 tr: © James Woodcock; tl: © Larry Mayer p. 97: © Larry Mayer. p. 98 © Robert Ekey. p. 100 br: © Larry Mayer. p. 101 burnt forest: © Larry Mayer; bl: © Roosevelt Jet; br: © Bob Zellar. p. 103 tc: © Larry Mayer. p. 104 c: © National Geographic Society. p. 105: © Catherine Baumann for Scholastic Inc. pp. 122-123 bc: © Stanley Bach for Scholastic Inc. p. 123: © John Lei for Sholastic Inc. p. 124 bc: © Stanley Bach for Scholastic Inc. p. 125 bc, cr: © John Lei for Scholastic Inc.; tr: Stanley Bach. p. 126 br: © Stanley Bach for Scholastic Inc. p. 127 bl: © Stanley Bach for Scholastic Inc.; br: © John Lei for Scholastic Inc. p. 128 bc: © Tim Davis/Photo Researchers, Inc. p. 129 tc: © Comstock, Inc. p. 131 cl: © Robert Bennett/FPG International Corp. p. 132 ml: © Jon Gilbert Fox; bl: © Daniel Nichols. p. 133 © Culver Pictures Inc. p. 134 cr: © Fred McKinney/FPG International Corp. p. 135 tl: © Erica Lansner/Bettmann Archive; c: © Richard Megna for Scholastic Inc.; br: © Stephen Ogilvy for Scholastic Inc.

Illustrations: pp. 8-9, 56-57, 88-89: Jeff Faria; pp. 92, 102-103: Karen Minot.